London's Splendid Square Mile

This edition first published in 2016 by
Step Outside Guides.

ISBN 978-1-908921-06-2
Printed and bound in Great Britain by Hertfordshire Display plc

Acknowledgements
Thanks to everyone who has trialled this book, and helped us to hone it:
for the Bellingham family, the Welch family, Tracey Soor, Fiona Laverty, Carl & Naomi Schofield, Peter & Tara Cooper and Phoebe Skinner.

Special thanks to the following people:
Hellen Martin, for kind permission to use William Whiffin's photograph on page 14.
Lesley Cowland for the photograph of the Lord Mayor's Coach on page 30.
Bremont Chronometers for permission for our readers to sit in their ejector seat!
Georgina Brown at the Wax Chandlers' Guild for permission to use their crest.
Paul Jagger of City and Livery for his helpful comments and information about London guilds.
Alex Robertson for his helpful information about London guilds.

Every effort has been made to ensure that the information in this book is as accurate as possible at the time of going to press. However, details such as phone numbers and opening hours may change, and we suggest that you ring or check online in advance to avoid disappointment.
The authors and publishers can accept no responsibility for any loss, injury, or inconvenience sustained by any person as a result of information or advice in this guide.
Any view or opinions expressed in this book are solely those of the authors and do not necessarily represent those of the venues described.

London's Splendid
Square Mile

For Poppy and Lily

A step outside Guide

CONTENTS

5 Introduction

6 How to use your book

8 Fire and Fish

10 The Great Fire of London

13 Mice and Money

16 Rest-your-legs page

19 From Bank to Guildhall

22 The Guilds of London

25 From Guildhall to an
   Old Wall

28 Rest-your-legs page

31 Postman's Park

Travel Tips

Travelcards give unrestricted travel on buses, trains and the Underground any time after 9.30am on weekdays, and all day at weekends.

Tube maps are available free at every Underground station.

The Transport for London website is *www.tfl.gov.uk*

If there are road works or building repairs there may be a diversion. Just take this as part of London life, and enjoy the detours.

Introduction

Hello there - pleased to meet you! We are the City of London's cheese-loving mice, Cam and Bert. The City of London is the oldest part of London, founded by the Romans nearly two thousand years ago. The rest of London has grown up around it, and the City of Westminster has become part of London too, but 'the City', or 'the Square Mile' as it is also known, is still a very special place and we love living here.

The City has many fascinating stories, places and things to discover and today we are going to take you on a journey to discover some of our favourites. Of course we will take you to see where we live, too!

One way of finding out about the City's history is by reading the memorial tablets (square blue plaques) which you will come across during the day. They tell you about all sorts of places and people, and we have marked them on the maps to help you find them.

Turn to pages 6-7 and read them carefully (or Caerphilly! tee hee) to make sure you are ready, and off we go, to discover London's Splendid Square Mile.

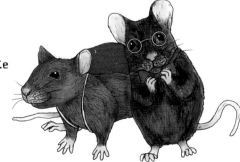

How to use your book

Pictures to help you find things

Good picnic spots

 Accessibility information for buggies and wheelchairs

City toilet scheme. Places showing this sign offer free use of their toilets

Things you can spot

A sticking-out clock is nearby. Draw a tick when you spot it

 A guild's hall is here

A City of London memorial tablet (blue plaque) is here

What to wear or bring with you

Your camera

Clothes and extras that suit the weather

Comfortable shoes

 Pencils and pens for *Rest-your-legs* pages

Binoculars if you have some

Your picnic

Useful information and accessibility

Church of St Magnus Martyr
Tues-Fri 10.00am - 4.00pm

The Walkie Talkie is free to enter, but it is essential to book in advance. *www.skygarden.london*

The Royal Exchange
Mon-Fri 10.00am - 6.00pm

Bank of England Museum
Mon-Fri 10.00am - 5.00pm
www.bankofengland.co.uk

Guildhall Art Gallery
Mon-Sat 10.00am - 5.00pm
Sun Noon - 4.00pm
www.guildhallartgallery.cityof london.gov.uk

Museum of London
Daily 10.00am - 6.00pm
www.museumoflondon.org.uk

Postman's Park
Daily 8.00am - Dusk

The annual Lord Mayor's Show, his parade through the City and the firework display are on the second Saturday in November.

Step-free access
Monument station and St Paul's station; nearest step free access is Bank Station, King William street entrance.

IMPORTANT SAFETY INFORMATION!

Remember that London is very big and very busy; drivers can be fast and impatient.
Only cross the road at traffic lights or pedestrian crossings.
Make sure your group stays close together
- no-one wants to get lost!

THE CORPORATION OF

Fire and Fish

THE CITY — OF LONDON

Starting Point:	Monument Station District and Circle Line
Finishing Point:	St Paul's Station, Central line
Walking Distance:	About 4 km
Time:	About 5 hours at a leisurely pace

Leave Monument station at the 'Fish Street Hill & Monument' exit. Look to the right and up, and there is The Monument, London's memorial to the Great Fire of 1666.

The Monument

If the column of the monument was laid on its side (in the right direction!) the ball of fire at the top would be at the exact spot where the Great Fire of London began.

The Fire was one of the most important events in The City's history. We tell you more about it on page 10.

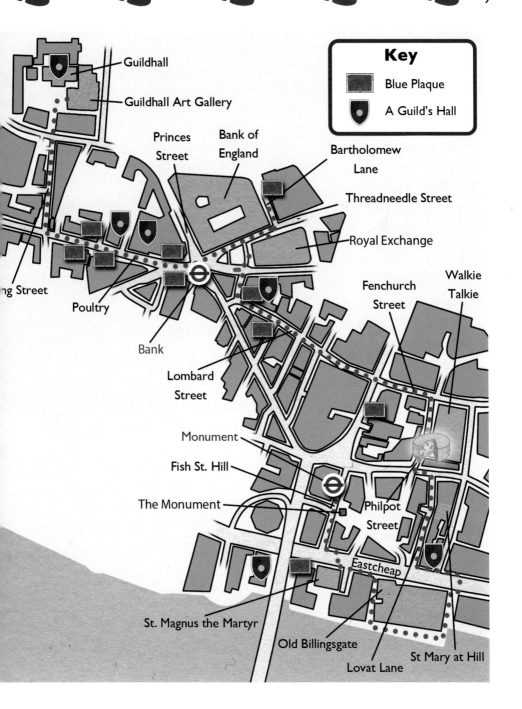

The Great Fire of

How the Fire started

How we know about it

In 1666 most of London was built of wood and wattle-and-daub (twigs and poles packed with clay and mud). The streets were narrow and the houses and shops were very close together. The fire started at 1.00 o'clock in the morning on the 2nd September in the shop of Thomas Faryner, the King's baker, who lived in Pudding Lane. Strong winds fanned the flames across The City, and it raged for four days and four nights, destroying four-fifths of the centre of London.

13,200 homes were burned down.

At this time Samuel Pepys (say Peeps) worked for the government. He kept a diary which tells us exactly what happened. This is what Pepys wrote about where we are standing right now:

"It began this morning in the King's baker's house in Pudding Lane, and it hath burned St. Magnus's Church and most part of Fish Street already. I rode down to the waterside... and there saw... poor people staying in their houses as long as till the very fire touched them and then running into boats."

Samuel Pepys buried his best cheese to save it from the fire. What a wise man!

London

After the Fire

After the Great Fire a law was passed that meant that any new buildings had to be made of stone, so there would never be another such terrible fire.

There was also a plan to completely redesign the City, with wide, straight streets. However, people whose homes and shops had been burned down refused to give up their land, and they built new homes and shops in exactly the same place as the old ones. This is why the City has windy, narrow streets. We think this makes it magical and mysterious – and much more fun to scamper through!

St. Magnus the Martyr, the church that Pepys mentions, was at one end of Old London Bridge and was rebuilt after the fire. It's just down Fish Street Hill from here. Can you see the clock sticking out? (✔) We want to take you there because there is a mouse-sized model of Old London Bridge inside. So let's go down the hill and over Lower Thames Street.

St. Magnus the Martyr

Open Tues – Fri 10.00 - 4.00, but as with all churches, may be closed for special services from time to time.
Fully accessible.

Just inside the church stands a fire engine. It is very old, but not quite old enough to have been of help in the Great Fire of London.

The model is in the main part of the church, on the left

Now we turn right out of the church, and right again. Very soon there is a 'Thames Path' sign, which we follow to the River Thames.

Thames Path

The river is the City's southern border. Let's turn left and walk alongside it. Beautiful Tower Bridge is ahead of us. Soon we come to an elegant yellowy brick building. This is Old Billingsgate market.

Old Billingsgate was London's fish market until 1982. Can you see two golden fish above the roof? They are wind vanes.

Turn left up the far side of Billingsgate. Cross the road then turn left again.

Mice and Money

W hen you reach a road called 'St Mary at Hill' stop and look along it to spot a sticking - out clock.

town as we scamper along it. Near the end is St Mary-at-Hill Church. If it's open, we can peek inside.

A few metres further on is a tiny road called Lovat Lane, which we turn into. This quaint road really makes us think of Old London

At the end of Lovat Lane is Eastcheap. Cross Eastcheap, turn left and then right into Philpot Lane. And this is where we live!

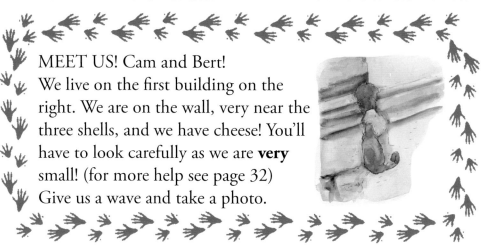

MEET US! Cam and Bert! We live on the first building on the right. We are on the wall, very near the three shells, and we have cheese! You'll have to look carefully as we are **very** small! (for more help see page 32) Give us a wave and take a photo.

Further along Philpot Lane is one of London's newest buildings, nicknamed the 'Walkie Talkie'. Facing it is our favourite place to play hide and seek - a vertical garden.

At the end of Philpot Lane, turn left into Fenchurch Street and walk straight across the junction to Lombard Street.

There is a sticking-out clock at St Edmund Martyr Church.

We love playing chase around the old signs hanging here. Can you guess which is our favourite? Can you spy the following signs:

- Crown
- King
- Cat & Fiddle
- Castle
- Anchor
- Grasshopper

Which do you like best?

William Whiffin took this photo of Lombard Street in 1926. Are any of the signs the same today?

Very near the end of Lombard Street on the right, we find Pope's Head Alley – what a funny name!

Turn right into the Alley. At the end, cross the road, then look back at the traffic island we have just used. The statue is of Henry Greathead. Not many people have heard of him, but he is an important figure in the story of London's public transport.

Meet Henry Greathead (1844 – 1896)

He is the inventor of the Travelling Shield which could bore wide tunnels under-ground.  This meant that the deep railway lines which we know as 'The Tube' could be bored. (Before that the under-ground railway was in a covered trench.)

The Royal Exchange

'The Bourse' (French for 'Exchange') was first built in 1565 as a business centre, including a courtyard where merchants could meet.

In 1571 Queen Elizabeth I commanded that it should be called the Royal Exchange. The building has been burned down twice, including once in the Great Fire of London.

We are now standing on the forecourt of The Royal Exchange. It is on our left as we look at Mr Greathead.

There are two sticking-out clocks here, one on each side of the Royal Exchange

It's time for a break to rest our legs now. There are loads of seats, so choose one and turn the page.

THE CORPORATION OF

Rest-Your-Legs

THE CITY OF LONDON

Above the main entrance to the Royal Exchange is the **tympanium** (the large triangle) which is filled with carved figures. If you've brought your binoculars, here's a chance to use them and have a really good look at this amazing sculpture that most people don't even notice!

Did you know there is only one road in the City of London? But there are many Streets and Alleys, and some of them have quite peculiar names. You could write any you have seen today in the spaces below, or you could even make up your own.

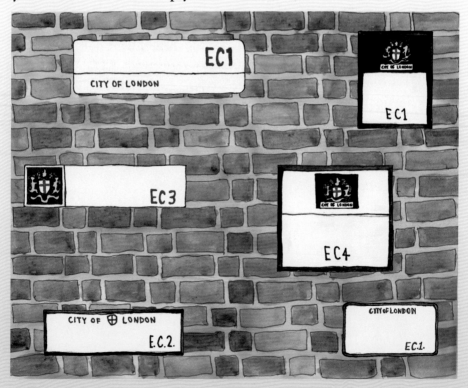

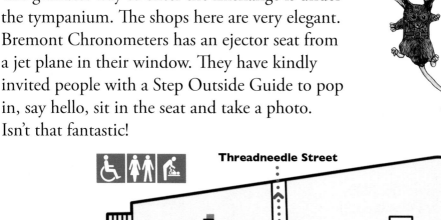

Are you rested and ready to visit the Royal Exchange? Hooray! Off we go.

The grandest way to enter the Exchange is under the tympanium. The shops here are very elegant. Bremont Chronometers has an ejector seat from a jet plane in their window. They have kindly invited people with a Step Outside Guide to pop in, say hello, sit in the seat and take a photo. Isn't that fantastic!

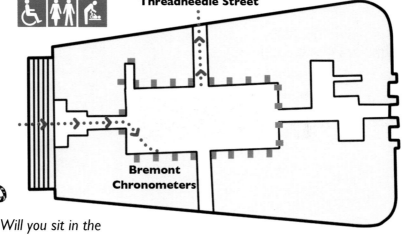

Threadneedle Street

Bremont Chronometers

Will you sit in the ejector seat?

Leave the Royal Exchange using the exit shown on the plan above. We are now facing the Bank of England, and we're going to visit it!

Cross Threadneedle Street by the zebra crossing to our right. The Bank of England Museum is just down Bartholomew Lane.

The Bank of England is the heart of 'the City'. It isn't a normal bank – it helps to look after the country's economy. It has HUNDREDS of gold bars in its **vaults** (cellars).

When we have finished at the museum, we return to Threadneedle Street. The Royal Exchange is opposite and Dick Whittington is high on its wall, to the right.

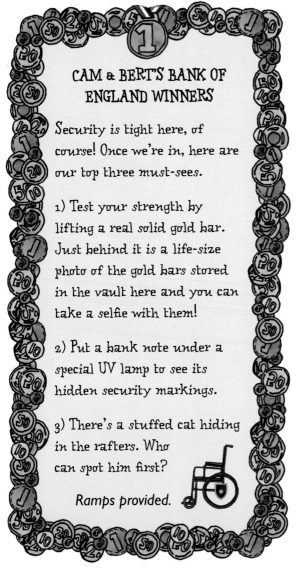

CAM & BERT'S BANK OF ENGLAND WINNERS

Security is tight here, of course! Once we're in, here are our top three must-sees.

1) Test your strength by lifting a real solid gold bar. Just behind it is a life-size photo of the gold bars stored in the vault here and you can take a selfie with them!

2) Put a bank note under a special UV lamp to see its hidden security markings.

3) There's a stuffed cat hiding in the rafters. Who can spot him first?

Ramps provided.

Meet Dick Whittington (about 1354 – 1423)

Did you know that Dick Whittington was a real person? Richard Whittington was Lord Mayor of London four times. He loved London, and Londoners, and he left most of his money to help the poor people in London. People still receive money from his bequest today, nearly 600 years later.

From Bank to Guildhall

We're going to turn right and walk down the side of The Bank of England. Cross Princes Street, ahead of us.

When you have crossed Princes Street, turn around and look at the Royal Exchange. Behind it you can see our favourite building, The Cheese Grater. Even we couldn't eat that much cheese!

Now turn back again. Across the busy junction to our left is Mansion House.

Mansion House

This grand building with its elegant columns and lamps is where the Lord Mayor of London lives. The Lord Mayor of London is not the same person as the Mayor of London. We will find out more about the Lord Mayor later.

Now walk down Poultry (see map on page 9). Number One Poultry is the pink and yellow striped building across the road. The stones have lovely swishy patterns in them. As we walk along Poultry, we can spy our next sticking-out clock, topped by a man carrying a huge ball on his back.

Meet Atlas from Greek Mythology

The ball Atlas is carrying is the world! He is on Atlas House, which was built for the Atlas Insurance Company in 1893. There is a bigger statue of Atlas above the door round the corner - we'll see that in a minute.

We are turning into King Street here, but before we turn, let's stand still and look further along the road. Can you spy another sticking-out clock? It's on the church of Saint Mary-Le-Bow.

As we turn into King Street we can see one of the oldest and most splendid buildings in the City. There it is, at the end of the street. It is Guildhall, and that is where we are going now.

Guildhall was the headquarters of medieval London's guilds. Let's pause in the courtyard here to read about them on the next three pages.

Guildhall was built over 500 years ago. It has survived the Great Fire and wartime bombings, and it is still a beautiful building today.

The Guilds of London

Medieval London was one of the world's most important centres of trade, and the guilds were at the heart of commercial life.

Each guild was run by one trade, and every craftsman had to belong to a guild, and had to pay to belong. In fact, the word 'guild' comes from Anglo-Saxon 'gildan' which means to pay. In return, the guild ensured that the craftsmen were properly trained, and that their work came up to the required standard. It also helped wages to remain steady and helped its members and their families if they suffered an accident or sickness.

The Queen is a member of the Drapers' Guild!

Dick Whittington was a member of the Mercers' Guild.

Sadly, there is no Worshipful Company of Cheesemakers - tee hee...

Guilds are also known as Livery Companies, and their title is 'Worshipful Company' or 'Honorary Company'.

There are guilds for air pilots and information technologists, glass sellers and fan makers, musicians and basketmakers – almost everything you can think of!

The twelve most important guilds are known as 'The Great Twelve'. Here they are:

1. The Worshipful Company of Mercers (general merchants)

2. The Worshipful Company of Grocers (spice merchants)

3. The Worshipful Company of Drapers (wool and cloth merchants)

4. The Worshipful Company of Fishmongers

5. The Worshipful Company of Goldsmiths (bullion dealers)

6 and 7. The Worshipful Company of Skinners* (fur traders)

7 and 6. The Worshipful Company of Merchant Taylors* (tailors)

8. The Worshipful Company of Haberdashers (clothiers in sewn and fine materials)

9. The Worshipful Company of Salters (traders in salts and chemicals)

10. The Worshipful Company of Ironmongers

11. The Worshipful Company of Vintners (wine merchants)

12. The Worshipful Company of Clothworkers

* The Skinners and Merchant Taylors argued so much about who should be ranked 6th, and who 7th, that in 1484 the Lord Mayor decided that each year they should swap round. They still do, and this is where the phrase 'all at sixes and sevens' comes from.

Today the guilds are still active and busy in the City of London, mainly with charitable work and enabling business men and women to meet. Thirty-nine of the guilds have their own halls, and we'll pass some of them today.

As we stand in the courtyard and face Guildhall, the Guildhall Art Gallery is on our right. It is open to the public and entrance is free, so let's pop in and see what we can find.

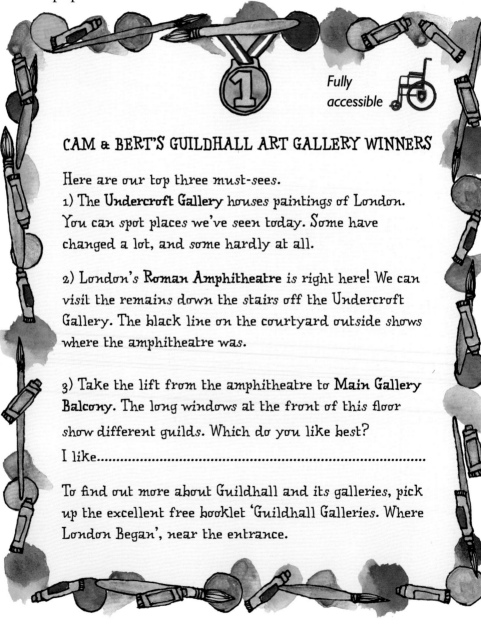

Fully accessible

CAM & BERT'S GUILDHALL ART GALLERY WINNERS

Here are our top three must-sees.

1) The **Undercroft Gallery** houses paintings of London. You can spot places we've seen today. Some have changed a lot, and some hardly at all.

2) London's **Roman Amphitheatre** is right here! We can visit the remains down the stairs off the Undercroft Gallery. The black line on the courtyard outside shows where the amphitheatre was.

3) Take the lift from the amphitheatre to **Main Gallery Balcony**. The long windows at the front of this floor show different guilds. Which do you like best?
I like..

To find out more about Guildhall and its galleries, pick up the excellent free booklet 'Guildhall Galleries. Where London Began', near the entrance.

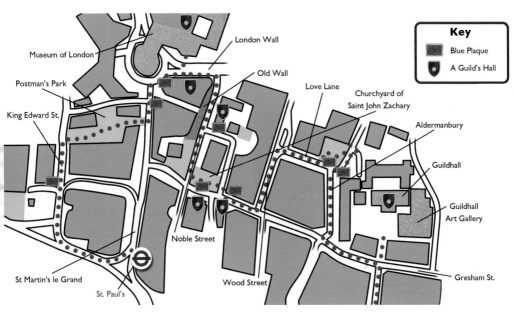

THE CORPORATION OF

From Guildhall to an Old Wall

THE CITY OF LONDON

Key

Blue Plaque

A Guild's Hall

Map labels: London Wall · Museum of London · Old Wall · Love Lane · Churchyard of Saint John Zachary · Aldermanbury · Postman's Park · King Edward St. · Guildhall · Guildhall Art Gallery · Noble Street · Gresham St. · St Martin's le Grand · Wood Street · St. Paul's

When we've left the gallery, follow the map above, past the church (St Lawrence Jewry) and pond.

Turn right along Aldermanbury. Near the end, on the right is a dribbly fountain. What is it made of? Let's go and take a closer look. On the other side of the road is a small garden. We are going up the steps to its left, and there we'll find a bust.

> The bust is of William Shakespeare, and it is here to honour two of his friends, who saved and published all his work. Hooray!

The church itself was destroyed by wartime bombing, and today people live in the tower. What a fun house!

Now let's walk down Wood Street, and then turn right into Gresham Street. We'll pass some of the halls that today's guilds still use.

> Most guilds' halls are quite new buildings because the great Fire, then The Blitz destroyed the old halls.

Walk past the statue and through to the knot garden – (it looks as if the bushes are tied in knots) – to Love Lane.

At the end of Love Lane we are going to turn left into Wood Street. Before that, on our right, can you see a church tower?

The coat of arms of the Worshipful

Across the road, just before Gutter Lane, is the Wax Chandlers' Hall. Their first hall was here over 500 years ago. This is their sixth hall.

> Wax chandlers traded in beeswax products, especially candles. Add their motto to their coat of arms below.

The very grand building next to Wax Chandlers' Hall is Goldsmiths' Hall. Opposite Goldsmiths' Hall, on our side of the road, is their garden.

It is in the old churchyard of St John Zachary. Let's take a look.

We love it! Go through the arch into the garden.

> On the low wall on the right there is a plaque which tells you how this special place was created by guilds working together.

Go down the steps at the end of the path to find the other part of the garden. It is a perfect place to take a break.

Company of Wax Chandlers

THE CORPORATION OF

Rest-Your-Legs

THE CITY ✠ OF LONDON

Can you design a stained-glass window for the Guildhall Art Gallery? You could even make up your own guild! We've drawn one for the Worshipful Company of Cheesemakers.

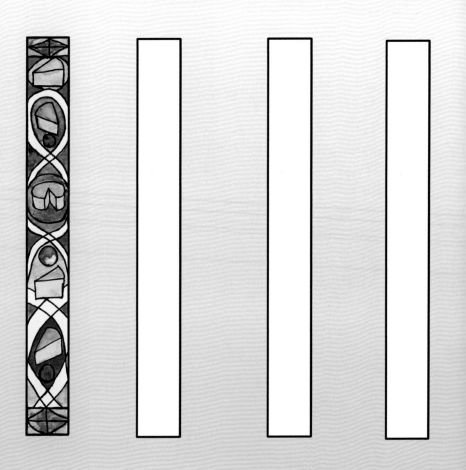

Now follow the map to the footpath, which runs along Noble Street and passes some of London's old walls.

Look down the first turning on the right (Oat Lane). The flag of the Pewterers' Guild flutters on their hall there.

The walls are Roman, Medieval and Victorian; there are plaques which tell you more about them. The big windows just past the third plaque belong to the Plaisterer's Hall. Although the building is not very old, its inside has been decorated in 18th century style. If we are lucky and the lights are on, we will be able to see inside.

At the end of Noble Street turn left. The splendid Museum of London is ahead of us.

The Museum of London is a fantastic place and it is free to visit. It tells the story of London from prehistoric times, right up to the present and even takes a look into the future.

It is a whole day out in itself and we hope you will go and see and experience all the wonderful things they have there on another day.

www.museumoflondon.org.uk

We are going to look at just one exhibit from the Museum today and we can see that from outside. Cross the road at the zebra crossing and on our right are large glass windows. Inside them is the Lord Mayor's coach.

The Lord Mayor's Coach

This enormous, fairy-tale coach is over 250 years old. It is kept here in the basement of the museum so that it can be wheeled onto the street easily.

Every November, a new Lord Mayor is elected by London's guilds to represent London throughout the world. The Lord Mayor's Show welcomes him or her into office with a grand parade through the City, and the Lord Mayor rides in this coach.

Sometimes we sneak a ride - look out for us if you are ever lucky enough to see the parade.

On the evening of the parade there is a free firework display on the River Thames!

Postman's Park

Now cross the road again on the same crossing and go down the street ahead of you, Aldersgate Street (this becomes 'St Martin's le Grand').

Cross this road at the first traffic lights and go into the tiny park which is next to the church. This is Postman's Park and it has a special secret.

POSTMAN'S PARK

This park got its name because postmen from the General Post Office headquarters nearby used to eat their sandwiches here.

Can you see the wall under the shelter ahead of you? This is **The Watts Memorial To Heroic Endeavour.** The tiled plaques there remember the stories of people, many of them children, who lost their lives trying to save others.

We think this fascinating and moving tribute is one of the best secrets in the City of London.

WILLIAM FREER LUCAS
·M·R·C·S· AT MIDDLESEX HOSPITAL
·L·L·D·
RISKED POISON FOR HIMSELF
RATHER THAN LESSEN ANY
CHANCE OF SAVING A
CHILD'S LIFE DIED
OC 1893·

Walk through to the other side of Postman's Park and turn left into King Edward Street. On our right, towards the end of the street, is Christchurch Greyfriars. It is another church destroyed by wartime bombs. A beautiful garden has been created in its place.

At the end of the road we turn left and ahead of us is St Paul's station, and there on our right is St Paul's Cathedral itself!

When we've crossed the road to the station it is time for us to leave you and get back to our cheese in Philpot Lane.

We've had a grate (tee hee) time with you today. We hope you enjoyed it too. Toodle pip, and as Samuel Pepys used to say,

and so to bed.

This picture shows you where we live (page 13)